Elemental Memoirs

Amberly Garcia

BookLeaf Publishing

India | USA | UK

Made with ❤ on the BookLeaf Publishing Platform
www.bookleafpub.in
www.bookleafpub.com

Dedication

To be of the stars, of fire, earth, and sea.
To be a breath of fresh air.
Such is the beauty of nature... and you.

Preface

This collection is a journey into the heart of the elements that shape our world and our souls. Through these poems, I invite you to explore the delicate balance of forces that exist beyond our understanding—the emotion of water, the power of fire, the quiet whispers of air, and the grounding nature of earth.

Each word is a reflection of something much greater than itself, a fleeting moment that carries the weight of eternity.

In these poems, you will find yourself in the flicker of stardust and the flow of rivers, in the warmth of sun and the stillness of the void. The symbols and metaphors woven throughout the pages are not merely artistic flourishes but a way of transcending the ordinary, inviting you to dive into the depths of the unseen, to touch the magic that lies within us all.

This book is a reflection of my own journey, as I, too, am made of the elements - *of stardust.*

It is a whisper to anyone who has ever felt the
pull of the elements within, beckoning them to
embrace the love and heartache of life.

Acknowledgements

To my Gram Emma. Thank you for being my sounding board and rock. For the laughter and for helping me become who I am. I would be lost without you.

Madre, thank you for encouraging me to read so much as a kid. You're the real MVP for taking me to all the bookfairs, because hey, that's what got me writing in the first place. Thank you for supporting me through the many phases of life.

Padre, thank you for always encouraging and supporting me. No matter where I have wanted to go in life, you're always right there, telling me I can do it. Thank you for showing me that kindness is strength. And for being there. Always.

Thank you to my siblings. But especially Daniel. Whenever I doubt myself, you're right there to listen and tell me how silly that is. You grieve my losses with me and celebrate my victories more than I do. Thanks for being my brother.

I have many many many friends to thank, but a
special thank you to the following:

Sasha! Thank you for being such a wonderfully
supportive friend! You're the first friend I shared
my writing with and your support has given me
courage to pursue it more purposefully.

Sarah! Thank you for always encouraging me!
And thank you for lighting a fire under me when
I need it! No matter the distance, I know you're
always there. I am forever grateful to have you in
my life. I'd be lost without your love and support!

Brittney! You've seen me through some of the
hardest times in my life. Thank you for giving
me support and love when I needed it most.

1. Elemental

I am of the Earth.
She grounds me,
Keeping me steady through uncertainty.

I am of the Flame.
He burns deep in my soul,
Refusing to let the spark die.

I am of the Air.
He's the fresh breath,
Reminding me that I am alive.

I am of the Sea.
She keeps me afloat,
Showing me I can rage, and still flow.

I am of the Spirit.
We are all, and nothing,
Alone and together, forever.

2. Fire-A Spark

Brown eyes wide with wonder,
Gazing at the inky night sky before her,
Expectation – She knows it will come.
The eagerness...
Just waiting... waiting.
Waiting for that sudden speck of light,
To give life to the hope in her chest.

Crow's feet now edge those brown eyes,
Gazing at the tasks before her.
Weariness – She feels the weight on her chest.
The exhaustion...
Just waiting... waiting.
Waiting for the day it feels easier.
She glances at the night sky, a speck up light fading.

A spark...

3. Earth-Home

Behind the curtain,
Of my mind's eye,
I can see clearly,
The watermelon sky.

I smell the sweet Earth,
As I bask in the rains,
I see jewel-toned sunsets,
Cascading the plains.

The heat starts to seep,
I run barefoot outside,
I hear chirping crickets,
The night sky opens wide.

I smell the green chile,
The leaves will soon change,
Picking pumpkins and movies,
Family costumes arranged.

I suddenly shiver,
At the stillness and cold.
But the Tumbleweed Snowman,
Stands proudly and bold.

I sneeze and I cough,
As the juniper blooms.
I brace for the windstorms,
And suddenly, BOOM!

I'm blown into summer,
And the sweltering heat.
The heavy monsoons,
The rain smells so sweet.

And as I look back,
And remember the seasons,
Remember the love,
And all of the reasons...

I find myself missing,
This place in my soul.
A piece of my heart,
That helps make me whole.

For though I might travel,
And though I might roam,

New Mexico Sunsets,
Will always be home.

5

4. Earth-Garlic

A sprinkle, a dash,
A dollop, a scoop.
No matter the pour,
Just know it is there.
That spicy aroma,
Sprinkled across her childhood.
It's in the spaghetti sauce,
A snowstorm piling,
Into the tomato red.
But it won't be ready till dad tries it.
It's in every spoonful,
With honey and lemon.
The ultimate cure,
For a sore throat.
It's at every barbeque,
hamburgers topped with cheese.
No matter the event,
Dad's at the grill, spice in hand.
Every home cooked meal,
Every birthday, Every laugh,

Every memory.
The scent of her youth,
Of love and family,
Of happiness.
It is home – *The spice of life.*

5. Earth-Waiting

Roots run deep,
Stretching into the soil.
I inhale the rich earth around me.

But there's something more, I know it.
I crave it.
I *need* it.

Something I've never seen before,
But I know it's there.
Waiting...

6. Spirit-Desire

What a strange thing it is,
To know deep in your bones,
There is something more.

It drives us forward,
Helping us to persevere,
Letting the pain and disappointment fade.

How can we crave something so deeply,
If we've never seen it before?
How can that be?

Unless it is *meant* to be.

7. Earth-Plucked

Nutrient rich soil,
A kiss from the Sun,
Tears of the Mother.
Breath of life inhaled.
She's born.
Petals reach for the sky,
Only to be plucked.

8. Spirit-Sweet Venom

I feel you,
Creeping into my veins.
Did you think I wouldn't notice?
The feel of you makes me shiver.

A smile touches my lips,
The thought of you seeping in.
And I chide myself.
It's a dangerous game.

Are you the cure to my jaded heart,
Or a venom in my veins?
Either way,
I can't help but drink you in.

9. Earth-Gravelike

Like a shadow,
Within a shadow,
It crept in very slow.
So stealthy,
I barely noticed,
So it had the chance to grow.

Within the dark,
It took my hand,
Before covering my skin.
The inky, muddy,
Serpent of dark,
I unknowingly let in.

It slithered across my body,
Like a dangerous cold,
Slick mud.
In the back of my mind,
I screamed and begged,
And asked myself to run.

But I halted,
At the familiar gaze,
Of the muddy serpent's eyes.
For I saw you,
And you saw me,
Soothing my surprise.

Until the fangs,
Broke through the muck,
Razor sharp and piercing.
I cried and wailed,
To no avail,
Your compassion was still missing.

And as you pierced,
My heart with fangs,
And wound around my throat.
The rest of me,
Was covered too,
With the lies that seemed to bloat.

They buried me,
Below the ground,
My screams could not be heard.
And suddenly,
The memories,

They began to blur.

The muddy serpent,
Unhinged its jaw,
And swallowed my whole soul.
A living grave,
I couldn't breathe,
I begged it would let me go.

Panic rose,
Within my throat,
My senses reawakened.
So I scraped and clawed,
And pulled myself,
From the grave dirt, now forsaken.

As I broke through,
The sludge and mud,
And breathed in the fresh air.
The snake,
It fell, a broken shell,
Nothing but despair.

For it had tried,
To smother me,
Misery loves company too.
But I am free,

No longer bound,
Not a broken piece of you.

15

10. Earth-Picked

So much time spent,
Making pretty petals,
Begging to be plucked.

Then you are picked,
And the joy quickly turns to dismay,
As you're put on display.

Petals wilt,
Leaves shrivel.
But you *wanted* to be picked.

I guess you assumed,
It would be every day.
Not just the once.

11. Fire-Burnout

Light me,
Let me bring light,
And give warmth.
I have so much to give.
I *need* to.
But I forget.
In my need to love,
I forget to temper the flames.
I forget to watch the wick.
I forget, and let myself burn out.
Till there is nothing of me left to give.

12. Air-Hell

Some say the world will end in Fire,
Some in Ice - Or so Frost said.
But I rather think the world will end with Air.
Strange, isn't it?
An element we can neither see, nor touch,
Yet, it is there all the same.
And like the other elements, we need it.
From that first breath of life, to the last.
The absence of it will leave us choking.
The stillness of it will lull us into a gentle calm.
The lack of it is the only way we know if it was there to
begin with.
It is isolation. A death.
That feels like hell to me.

13. Earth-Thorns

Such a delicate thing,
Soft and pretty.
Till they started to tear at my petals.

Was it vanity?
Jealousy?
Neglect?

It doesn't matter.
Screw the pretty petals.
I've got thorns now.

I *dare* you to pick me.

14. Earth-Winter

In the dead of winter,
Breathe.
Remember to rest.
It is okay.
Spring will come again,
And new life will bloom.
Don't rush it.
You are recovering.
Preparing.
New life will come.
And when it does,
Remember to breathe.

15. Spirit-Worth It?

What if this is it?
What if, despite all the effort,
All the pain, all the hurt,
What if this is it?

Was it worth it?
Getting to experience all of this?
There is so much I wanted.
So much I *needed.*

But when I think back to my mom's laugh,
My dad's smile.
The peace I felt,
Having my siblings safe in my arms.

Unequivocally, yes.

Despite all the pain this life has to offer,
The love... The love I have felt in this life,

Even if I lose it all,
It was worth it.

16. Spirit-Warrior

Show me those pretty scars,
Let them breath and be proud.
For it means you survived.

Show me the battles you fought.
Show me your bleeding heart,
And I'll show you mine.

My scars run deep - rivers carved,
Practically tearing my heart apart.
But it still beats.

Yes, it hurts,
But it is a reminder that I am a warrior.
And so too are you.

17. The Sun and Moon

To be the Sun,
Must be such a beautiful thing.
The warmth, the light,
To bask in it must be incredible.

But I've never been the Sun.
And I guess that's okay.
I think I'd rather be the Moon.
She is soft, and gentle.

She never forces,
Those born in a little darkness,
To feel bad for not shining as brightly,
Or to *bask* in the light.

I like the calmness, despite the power.
While the Sun and the Flame are one,
The Moon and the Sea are too.
They flow through me, a gentle guide.

18. Sea-Heart of Mine

Delicate as seafoam,
She cannot stay hidden.
As much as she'd like to hide,
Her depths *crave* to be caressed.

Dive in,
I promise she'll be gentle.
There is rage beneath the surface,
But it's all passion and grief.

Touch her gently,
And the rage will ebb,
Into a crashing wave,
Of never ending love.

Ride the wave,
And do not try to tame the Sea.
For she is a powerful,
And you'll never be the same.

Are you brave enough,
To be consumed by her?
She'll take you to new depths and heights,
That heart of mine.

19. Earth-A Gentle Touch

I eye you with dismay,
Pity in my heart,
As you extend your hand.

Do not be lured in,
By the siren's call,
Of pretty rose petals.

I'm all thorns now.
And I promise,
I *do* fight back.

But your fingers,
They caress me,
And I don't know what to do.

No prick of my thorns,
For you did not try to pluck me.
Merely, a gentle touch...

20. Spirit-Raven Wings

Carry me on Raven wings,
Across the inky sky.
Let the moonlight seep,
Deep into my bones.

I feel the wind,
Caress my skin,
Guided by the stars.
But where?

I gaze up,
Lost in the stardust,
And it just gazes back.
I think I'm finding her.

That woman I used to be,
She's buried deep,
Beneath broken shards,
I feel her.

She's changed so much,
Her scars shine in the starlight.
But she's there.
Brave, brave woman.

I embrace her,
A thanks,
And she fades -
Stardust once more.

I breathe a sigh of relief,
How long? *How long,*
Had I carried that grief?
My heart feels light once more.

And then I know,
I can see where we are heading,
Carried gently,
On Raven wings.

21. Spirit-Stardust

I am stardust,
The magic of the Universe.

Look into my eyes,
A nebula will gaze back.

Delve into my mind,
You'll find a cosmic web.

There is lightning in my veins,
And an inexplicable hope in my chest.

And when the Universe speaks to me,
In a language I don't know how to speak,

I can't help but to breath in peace.
I don't know what she says, but I understand her.

In the same way I just know myself.
Because we are the same.

www.ingramcontent.com/pod-product-compliance
Lightning Source LLC
LaVergne TN
LVHW010927200726